Face the Dawn
DEVOTIONS FOR ADVENT

© 2022 Rich Lambert

All rights reserved.

Published in Jacksonville, Florida by Bible Study Media, Inc.
Cover and Interior design by Shelby Dinkel of Dinkel Digital, LLC.

ISBN # 978-1-942243-64-9
Library of Congress Control Number: 2022917608

No part of this publication may be reproduced, stored in a retrieval system, or transmitted in any form or by any means electronic, mechanical, photocopy, recording, or otherwise except for brief quotations in printed reviews, without the prior written permission of the publisher.
www.biblestudymedia.com.

All Scripture quotations are from the ESV® Bible (The Holy Bible, English Standard Version®), copyright © 2001 by Crossway, a publishing ministry of Good News Publishers. Used by permission.
All rights reserved.

Printed in the United States of America.

For Jennifer, of course.

And for S+K Hughes, P+E Lee, and J+K Shanks –
friends who make The Dawn feel nearer.

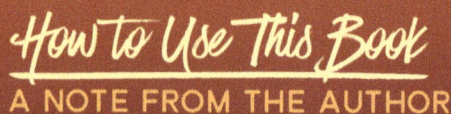

How to Use This Book
A NOTE FROM THE AUTHOR

This book is a map, drawn to help you settle into a seasonal place of residence, *Advent*. Maps give us a sense of direction and place, so we feel less like strangers and more like locals.

This map is built on four main highways into this new locale—the four Sundays of Advent along with the four weeks that trail after them. Each highway has four side streets that branch off from it—the four Scripture passages assigned to each Sunday according to the Revised Common Lectionary. These four Sunday readings are the subject and source of the daily devotionals for the week following, which creates a bit of a math problem. With four weekly Scripture passages and seven days to a week, there aren't enough passages to match the number of days. It's the old hot-dog-and-bun conundrum. So, for three of the days each week, a cul-de-sac is constructed out of a repeated text, where we look at a different aspect of the same text. If cul-de-sacs aren't to your taste, you can always drive past them and skip the detour altogether. If you do turn in, the nice thing about cul-de-sacs is, if you just follow them all the way around, eventually they bring you back out to the main road.

A few more thoughts on repetition. For some reason, modern readers feel cheated by it. They feel like they are being sold used goods instead of something new and unspoiled. That is a bias I think we should work hard to break, and here are just a few reasons why:

1. Every passage of Scripture is an ocean we could spend a lifetime exploring and still not discover it all. Repetition in Scripture reading is an act of diving deep and expecting to find new wonders floating just a little deeper than we were able to reach on previous dives.

2. Repetition is to Christian meditation what inhaling is to breathing. So, breathe deep.
3. Repetition is the lost tool of pedagogy. It is a refiner's tool.
4. If Scripture is spiritual food for the soul, chew slowly. Savor the feast.

How did we decide which passages to repeat? Author's choice. It was entirely arbitrary. For days that needed a borrowed text, I wrote about whatever I found in that week's readings that bothered or puzzled me, what seemed strange and out of place, what took my breath away, or what left me in tears. I read these verses over and over and over again. I wrung myself out in prayer, and then I tried to follow the Holy Spirit across the keyboard, hoping to find what my heart needed most and trusting that your heart might need something very much the same.

Now that the map is in your hands, how you use it falls entirely to the discretion of the mapholder. You can walk and measure every square inch of this neighborhood like the town surveyor. You can amble and wander, routeless, like a dog-walker at the end of a long day. You can visit the same site twenty-eight days in a row and never make it from one end of this map to the other. It doesn't matter, so long as you trust the Spirit of God to show you around the place and expect to find the Lamb of God around every corner. However you spend your time here, the goal is to make Advent feel less like a rest stop and more like home.

Rich Lambert

Table of Contents

Introduction — 09
HOLIDAY IN EXILE: ADVENT AS A WAY OF LIFE

Week 1 — 13
GOD BRINGS US THROUGH JUDGMENT INTO SALVATION BY HIS SON

Week 2 — 35
GOD BRINGS US THROUGH CONFLICT INTO THE KINGDOM IN HIS SON

Week 3 — 59
GOD BRINGS US THROUGH EXILE TOWARD HOME THROUGH HIS SON

Week 4 — 83
GOD BRINGS US THROUGH PROPHECY TO FULFILLMENT THROUGH HIS SON

Introduction
HOLIDAY IN EXILE: ADVENT AS A WAY OF LIFE

Advent is a celebration of home in a place far removed. It is a holiday of homesickness. Thirty years ago, I spent the Fourth of July with a handful of expatriates in Australia. We tried to mimic the celebrations of our childhood as best we could. We barbecued in the backyard, decorated cupcakes with stars and stripes, and tied red, white, and blue balloons to the backs of the patio chairs. We even invited a few Aussies to join us—who mostly stood around politely holding plastic American flags and wondering what all the fuss was about.

There were no marching bands thumping and tooting John Philip Sousa, no lawn chairs lined up along parade routes, no classic convertibles rolling down the boulevard with a bespangled Asparagus Queen, or Onion Queen, or Apple Queen, or other farmland dignitary perched atop the backseat. There were no VFW color guards in garrison caps and vests covered in patches and pins, no kids with patriotic streamers woven through bike spokes, no buntings draped over balconies, no flags hanging from the lampposts, and no fireworks after sundown. Our ad hoc holiday sputtered and fizzled out faster than a dime store sparkler. *It's hard to hold onto home when you are a world away.*

If we hadn't noticed the date on the calendar, we might have let the day pass without any celebration. We didn't *have* to stage a holiday where none existed. We could have treated it like any other day. Nothing would have come of it. We wouldn't have lost our citizenship or been barred from all subsequent Fourth of July celebrations. We wouldn't have been turned back at the customs gates upon our return home. No one would have known. But we knew. And in that sense, we *did* have to celebrate, flimsy as it might have been. We had to celebrate because home was part of us. We had to celebrate because home would always be part of us. It's hard to hold onto home when you're a world away, but it is even harder not to hold on at all.

Advent takes center stage on the church calendar between Thanksgiving and Christmas, but we do ourselves a great disservice when we think of it as locked away in a particular season. Advent can't be captured and kept in just four weeks. Advent is the continual ache for the home that is part of us. Advent is the admission that our bodies and lives are here, but our hearts are someplace else. In that strange and holy discomfort, our bodies and lives are meant to catch up to our hearts and reflect our true home as well. We are reaching for that home from a great distance, and Advent helps us shape our true identity (Philippians 3:20). Advent is the admission and celebration that we are *missionary exiles*.

As **exiles,** we will live the rest of our earthly lives in this place. We are called to inhabit a particular time, location, and condition. To inhabit means to dwell inside an experience. We are intimate and familiar with it. We feel and share the blessings and graces that occur here. We are part of them and can attest to them. They belong to us. But we can say the same about the sufferings that happen here. They belong to us, too. To be exiles means that we are residents here. We live here, for now.

As **missionaries,** we come from someplace else. We have been sent, and we bring a message of hope not known to this place. Our exile here is not for punishment but for proclamation—to share the good news that Jesus Christ has entered this world, lived faithfully in it, died sacrificially for it, and risen gloriously to re-create it. Someday he will return to make this re-creation lasting and final. In the waiting, we hold to the truths of the Gospel and the promises of this hope:

1. Your sufferings are real and are constant reminders that we can't be gods to ourselves.
2. The good things you enjoy are real, too, but limited—and far less than what God has in store for those he has made his children.

What a proclamation! God would give you more than all your sufferings and blessings in Jesus.

As **missionary exiles,** we don't quite belong here. We don't fit. This place is our home for now, but Christ is bringing us a home for all eternity. And we know the difference. The more the kingdom of Jesus grows and comes alive in us, the less we are welcome here. The ways of this world are passing away, and the ways of the new heaven and new earth are breaking through. We live in this place, and we love it—all while we are letting go of it at the same time. That makes us stand out like strangers. And we are. God put us here as *"strangers and aliens"* for that very purpose (Ephesians 2:19).

Next, there's the matter of language. As missionary exiles, we speak a mixed language. We speak the language of here and home at the same time. The language of the kingdom spoken during our exile cannot be all "Yes!" We cannot be too settled here. But also, the language of our exile cannot be all "No!" We cannot be too disconnected here—as if we've already left this world and its cares behind. The language of our exile—the language of kingdom Christians in the world that Jesus is judging and redeeming—is a constant "yes, but no." And that is the most offensive language we could possibly speak. We are always loudly affirming the inbreaking of grace, and we are always loudly denouncing the old strongholds of death. Our neighbors outside the church, and inside it too, would rather we speak one of these extremist languages because they are predictable and resistible. But *our* language is always challenging, always calling for growth and renewal, just like redemption. Just for opening our mouths and raising our voices, we invite hostility.

But for kingdom people, for Advent people, for homesick Christians, we can't help it. Even though we've never seen our true home, it grows larger in our hearts day by day. It grows larger in our speech and actions, too. As our missionary work for our neighbors becomes more earnest, so does our longing for home. And as our ache for home becomes more urgent, so does our missionary work while we wait. Our work and waiting are inseparable, just as they were for Noah the ark-builder, John the Baptist, Isaiah the prophet, David the psalmist, Paul the apostle, and James the brother of Jesus—all of whom are waiting for us in the pages of this book.

Advent is a homesick holiday. The balloons are half-deflated. The cupcakes are melted. The streamers and banners sag and droop, the fireworks wheeze and rasp, and when we sing the songs of home, we mutter them under our breath because our voices crack and break when we sing from the heart. But we keep the holiday because any day now, the full holiday will break through. Our home longs for us even more than we long for it.

Happy Advent.

Week 1

GOD BRINGS US THROUGH JUDGMENT INTO SALVATION BY HIS SON

Isaiah 2:1–5; Romans 13:11–14; Psalm 122; Matthew 24:36–44

DAY 1 – ISAIAH 2:1–5
The Highest Mountain

"How will you know the last days have come?" Isaiah the prophet calls down through the ages. "Watch for the mountains to be rearranged, like kids choosing sides on the playground at recess, and the mountain of the house of the Lord is everyone's top pick." Of all the peaks that tower over the Earth—Denali, Kilimanjaro, Everest, Meru—Zion will rise above them all (Isaiah 2:3, paraphrase).

Zion is the mountain on which God's temple was built in Jerusalem, so Zion became shorthand for the place where God dwells, the site of God's throne, or the place where God rules. The trouble with Isaiah's claim is that none of the so-called mountains of Jerusalem are very impressive. They are elevated ground, but as mountains go, they make alpinists yawn. They are squat and stumpy hills, dunes practically.

What is shocking about Isaiah's forecast is the very un-mountainous way he speaks of Mount Zion. He uses a future passive voice: it "shall be established as the highest of mountains, and shall be lifted up above the hills" (2:2). Any reader who has ever been on a hike knows that this is not how mountains work. They don't fluctuate; they don't accordion. By nature, mountains are fixed. When tectonic plates stop shifting, mountains stand still, sky-scraping or stunted, and don't change ranks. Have you ever heard of a mountain being hoisted up? Have you ever seen a mountain lifted until its peak soared above its rivals?

Isaiah is not being literal, of course. He is drawing for us a map of spiritual topography. Isaiah is a prophet who speaks in word-pictures to communicate otherworldly visions and theological mysteries. When he forecasts that Zion will be established as the highest of the mountains, lifted above the hills, he is not calling for the mountain to expand, telescope, or levitate. He uses this image to mean that in the last days, the rule of God will be exalted in the hearts of many peoples, and in the last days, the nations will prefer his government and guidance to all others (2:2–3).

Why has Zion, the smallest of hills, the most disregarded of mountains, been awarded this new stature? Because every other government on Earth has failed. Every. Last. One. Not one of them has panned out. It's not that they've suddenly all vanished or evaporated. The mystery of this passage is that the governments of the world are still up to their usual games of statesmanship. They are all still holding forth from their royal palaces, capitol buildings, parliament houses, and oval offices. They are still running for election, contesting vote counts, being inaugurated, honoring treaties, signing accords, caucusing, legislating, decreeing, condemning, threatening, passing sanctions, and mobilizing armies to violate or defend borders.

Meanwhile, the kingdom of God—established in Christ and hidden within the nations and the peoples—looks beyond magistrates, politicians, and officials. Earthly powers may offer security and stability in some guise, but they cannot and do not offer what the heart truly craves. They cannot govern for reconciliation, healing, or renewal (2:4). But Zion can.

With his law, God has decreed that sin is judged. With his word, he has declared sinners forgiven. His way is the atonement of the cross, and his paths of life run straight through the empty tomb. Zion has decreed that the rejected are claimed, the old is made new, the dead are raised to life, and believers are promised a lasting, unbreakable peace, making every dispute in this life seem trifling. In the fully realized kingdom of Jesus, we will give up our gerrymandered conflicts and repurpose weapons into garden tools. We won't remember combat tactics because we will no longer be trained fighters—we will be professional worshipers. That calling begins now, in anticipation of Christ's return.

But how do we do it? How do Advent people live in a politicized world?

How do we stream past the politicians and pundits and flow to Zion with the other kingdom citizens?

- Cast your vote, but don't cast your heart into the ballot box with it.
- Measure every partisan claim by the mystery of the Gospel, lived, taught, and blessed by Jesus. Sacrifice is gain, weakness is strength, and emptiness is fullness. You are alive in this mystery alone.
- Spend more time listening to the voice of the Holy Spirit in Scripture than you do listening to voices in newscasts and roundtables. Literally track the time you spend listening to each.
- When others talk politics and positions, you talk theology and Gospel.
- Root your expression of identity in the kingdom of Jesus more than you establish it in party and country.

At the end of these verses, Isaiah exhorts, *"O house of Jacob, come, let us walk in the light of the LORD"* (2:5). We might paraphrase it this way: "Keep Zion in front of you, and don't stop walking. Jesus will meet us on the way."

Faith and practice: Which are you more passionate about: another victory for your political tribe or the return of Jesus? Doesn't another win by our political tribes keep us from needing Jesus to return quickly? What political divisions existed among Jesus's twelve? Which political agenda from among his twelve did Jesus favor? Does that suggest any adjustment to your thinking and practice?

DAY 2 – ROMANS 13:11–14
Wear the Light

The return of Jesus is no surprise, says Paul, because the Lord's nearness is written all over you—you wear his nearness like a suit of clothes. Paul insists that what you believe about the coming of the Lord and its closeness is not an inner secret. You wear the cosmological countdown in your conduct.

Salvation is nearer to us now than it has ever been, Paul reminds us. *"The night is far gone; the day is at hand"* (Romans 3:11–12). So wear it. Wear the morning. Wear the brightening dawn. Take off the garments of darkness. Take off the old ways of immaturity, childishness, selfishness, and hoarding. Everything that Paul includes in his strange list that follows is an act of indulgence, excess, and gluttony. These are the fearful reflexes of running low and going without—a bottomless gobbling done from worry that God isn't, after all, generous from his good pleasure and love. It's that anxious gulping that Paul calls sleep, darkness, night.

Faith, on the other hand, believes that God is good. He gives us all we need every day. Many days, he gives us beyond what we need. He gives us from his more. He gives us what we don't have words to ask for or imagination to dream up, Paul says in another of his letters (Ephesians 3:20). Believing this, faith has no need to take for itself, to scrounge and scrabble and stockpile. For faith, there is only rejoicing and trusting and receiving. And when we don't receive, because from his goodness he has not given, we can still rejoice.

The good news is that God doesn't expect us to rid ourselves of our own darkness or manufacture our own light. He dresses us in the perfect work of Jesus, and the cross and resurrection are our change of clothes. In the occupied cross and the empty tomb, we trade darkness for light, again and again, with repentance and confession and alleluias and amens.

This God is not chintzy. He is not cheap or refusing. He has emptied our emptiness in the cross and filled us with his fullness in the resurrection.

The result, assures Paul, is that you are the cosmological map, the ticking clock that counts down the nearness of Christ Jesus. When people see that you do not live to feed appetites that can't be satisfied, they will know that you are filled with something expansive and lasting. They may even start to crave it for themselves.

Faith and practice: How (specifically) will you wear light today? Monitor yourself throughout the day, so the light doesn't slip or fade with fatigue and carelessness. And remember, we wear light because of joy in the nearness of Jesus's return, not from fear of judgment.

DAY 3 – ROMANS 13:11–14
Face the Dawn

Biblically speaking, if asleep is forgetfulness, then awake is remembering. Asleep is oblivious, and awake is expectant. Asleep is an exit—from activity, responsibility, pressures, and problems. Awake is a bold walking out to meet what approaches. Asleep is a kind of hiding, a peering out between the blinds, but awake is a watchman.

And so Paul writes this section of his letter to the Roman church as a spiritual rousing, a theological shaking awake. "Besides, you know the times," writes Paul. "This is not the time to drift in dreams, unaware of unfolding realities. This is the time to be alert and attuned to the swell of salvation—it is nearer now than ever. Jesus is about to step through the realms in a flourish of reconciliation, restoration, and shalom."

Who would want to be lost in a detached fog when Christ returns? It would be like dozing through your own birth, snoring through your wedding day, or snoozing through the festivities of Christmas morning while everyone else is downstairs unwrapping gifts and clinking eggnog toasts.

After all, when the Holy Spirit whispered belief and repentance into our hearts, wasn't that a waking? When we stood beneath the cross and breathlessly grasped that the crucified Jesus is our guilt offering and our debt of righteousness paid in full, wasn't that a waking? When we ran to the vacant tomb after the women on the third day to hear its echoes of eternal peace and unshakable acceptance, wasn't that a waking? Isn't it also a waking to turn our backs on the fading night of unbelief as we turn ourselves into dawn-facing saints who look for his return? Isn't all our worship dawn-facing?

In baptism,
and in eucharist,
and in singing,

and in tithing and giving,
and in preaching, prayer, and liturgy,
and in repentance, forgiveness, and peace-making,
and in love of neighbor and encouragement to the brothers and sisters—
isn't all this a shaking to wakefulness?

Perhaps what's most shocking about passages like this is how Christians insist on reading them as bristling warnings of doom and not as the laughing reminders of promise they were intended to be. What's at stake here is not being caught unready at Jesus's appearing and swept away in judgment. What's at stake is hope—hope in the meantime, hope in the waiting, hope in the face of whatever comes next.

Hope allows us to read our times through the lens of revelation and prophecy rather than through circumstance and news reports. Hope allows us to taunt the darkness around us and say without flinching, "Darkness, you are losing. Healing is almost here." It's the ability to wave off the sleep of selfishness while saying, "Something far better is on the way." It's a foreign language that most folks won't even begin to understand, but you should speak it anyway, if only to yourself.

And you should continue to live like the night is slipping and the day is soaking through. Be ready to witness and welcome the dawn—like a rooster clearing his throat and gulping a lungful of breath to announce the day. So wake up! Stay awake! Wake up again!

Faith and practice: What current sleepiness do you need to wake from? What dawn-facing, dawn-announcing activity would transform today from the routine to the eternal?

DAY 4 – PSALM 122
A Song Just Out of Reach

Of all the trophies lining King David's case, none glittered brighter than Jerusalem. It had been a Jebusite stronghold, so impregnable that no one thought it would ever change hands. That is until David and his God took it away from them, and David named the place after himself to seal the exchange. The City of David, he called it. Despite what it may seem, David was not over-crediting himself, because every Jew in the land, and every Jew-hater at the border, knew that any victory of David was a victory for David's God. That's how it worked among nations and kingdoms in the ancient world. There was a lot of taunting back and forth to the tune of, "Our god is better than your god." Whoever won the battle, of course, got to keep singing, because the better god prevailed. And Yahweh never lost, unless he threw the fight on account of the people's sin. On this occasion, however, God's sun-bright smile burned over David, and overnight, Jerusalem went from being a Jebusite stronghold to a Jewish one.

To show that he and Yahweh were madly devoted to one another, David hoisted his flag over the city walls and danced around the Ark of the Covenant—that strange, acacia wood and gold-overlaid box on which sat the mysterious presence of the Lord. David celebrated all the way into the center of town in a holy frenzy. Later, Solomon, David's son and successor, would build a temple for the presence of God to reside in. Everyone knew that the City of David would be God's new address for the foreseeable future.

But David's victory did expose a weakness. If David could conquer the city once, who was to say that another conqueror couldn't arise and take it back again? And so David wrote a song, and the people sang it until their throats went hoarse and raspy. "Peace for Jerusalem!" they bellowed, "Peace, and endless peace! Peace within your walls means more worship to Yahweh! Lock your enemies out, and our worship will never fade!"

It's a song we don't sing much anymore. One reason the tune is forgotten is that the presence of God has spread across the earth in the outpouring of his Spirit, and he resides in a living temple now. Another reason is that our experience matches Paul's. Paul writes to his churches that peace is nice but not necessary. Whether stoned, flogged, beaten, banished, or locked away in stocks in the dungeon basement, we will praise God anyway for his marvelous salvation in Christ Jesus. Nothing can impede the grace of Jesus to us; nothing can stop our worship of him. Even stopping our breath will only speed the day when we worship him in person and praise his name. The only thing sweeter than worship in a season of peace, says Paul, is worship when all the chips are down, and our backs are to the wall. Worship is best when it's desperate.

The song won't be forgotten for much longer, however. We will sing an updated version when Jesus returns for us (Revelation 21:25). "Peace in the New Jerusalem!" we will sing, "Endless peace! Peace upon peace upon peace. Guilt and shame are gone. Death is no longer. The deceiver and accuser is vanquished. We have no more enemies, within or without, for Christ the lamb is victorious. Leave the city gates open! Break their locks and lose the keys. Christ, our eternal peace has brought us to live with him forever!"

In all our joyful, hopeful Advent waiting, it's like an old song we used to know, humming on our lips, murmuring over our tongues, stirring in our hearts, calling to be learned all over again. It's a song just out of reach, but not for much longer.

Faith and practice: What makes your worship desperate? Describe, out loud or in writing, the moments that prepare you for the return of Jesus and the age of endless peace.

DAY 5 – PSALM 122
Glad

Of all the places that once captivated David's heart, his hometown of Bethlehem—the sheep meadows, the victorious battlefield, the palace halls—no place held a tighter grip on him than the house of the Lord, the place where people gathered to be renewed in God's presence. *Glad* is how he describes it, and you get the sense that David is belting out in the opening bars of this song, "There's no place I'd rather be!" without so much as a hint of churchy and sanctimonious exaggeration.

Our language for church isn't as shiny and new. It's often a secondhand and haggled language. We use words like *should, ought,* or even *need*. Sometimes we let slip an occasional *have-to*. We go to church hoping but not expecting, whereas David's pockets and heart were spilling over with expectation. *Glad*, David sings.

And why would he not be glad, after all David's been through? From soaring heights to scandalous failures, God loves him still. The faith of a saint and the flesh of a playboy, and God loves him still. A warrior king who'd die for his troops and a mafia boss who orders a hit on one of his own lieutenants, yet God loves him still. The shepherd king of youthful strength is now aged and fading, and God loves him still. The father of the year is now hunted by a throne-hungry son, and God loves him still.

Glad, David sings, because he is certain that when his merry parade finally winds its singing, chanting way through the streets of Jerusalem to the Temple, the doors won't be slammed shut on them and barred, and the gates won't be chained and locked. The place will be wide open, ready to receive them with an eternal welcome. David is glad to be in God's presence because God is glad first. That's the only reason any of us ever has for going to church. *"There thrones for judgment were set,"* David sings in verse 5, without flinching, because he knows that this God of perfect holiness and righteousness chooses to judge with equally perfect mercy and grace for the utterly helpless and humble! David can dance through the streets to the house of the Lord because the one who presides there loves us with his best, even when we are at our worst.

David didn't know the resurrection like we do, of course, and yet he knew it better than most. He felt the dead-end deadness of sin and had life breathed back into him with the holy kiss of God himself. You can almost trace the shape of the cross and the vacant tomb in the verses of this song!

And when you're done tracing, you should start singing your own gladness. But not just on your way to church. Your joy should reach past church all the way to the return of Jesus. For us, this is an Advent song. "Jesus is coming, and it will be the day of our gladness!" we can sing. "When the call of his arrival goes out, we will dance out to meet him! He has kissed away our guilt with his grace. He has answered our repentance with rejoicing!" Thanks to David, we also know what Jesus's own disposition will be on the day of his coming, and every day after, through the eternal ages.

Glad.

Faith and practice: What is your disposition toward worship and the return of Jesus? If you are not glad, something is wrong. You are probably trying to earn in some way what only grace can give. Grace always gives gladly.

DAY 6 – MATTHEW 24:36–44
In the Days of Noah

Judgment is coming, just like in the days of Noah. But mercy comes with it, just like in the days of Noah. The only ones who should feel dread at these verses aren't listening to them, just like in the days of Noah. They laugh at the warnings and yawn at the invitations—and then the skies darken and open like floodgates, just like in the days of Noah.

But Noah believed. Noah stands in the heart of these doom-soaked verses like a Colossus of good news (Matthew 24:38). Noah believed that the God who revealed himself was a just God and fully within his right to judge sin of all kinds and degrees. So Noah followed the strange blueprints God gave him and laid out stacks of lumber in the outline of a great ship. Noah also believed that the God who revealed himself was merciful and entirely within his right to provide an escape from the judgment he was sending. So Noah told his sons to strap on their tool belts and meet him at the lumber-filled vacant lot just east of town first thing in the morning.

It's not as if they kept their strange construction project a secret. Day after day, they measured and fitted and joined. Day after day, they hammered and sawed and swabbed pitch on the hull. Day after day, the structure looked less like a barn and more like a frigate. How long did it take? How many weeks? How many months? How many years? If you build a yacht from keel to cabin in the middle of the desert, eventually the neighbors will notice.

What's shocking is not that the rains fell in waves, and the waters rose as quick as drawing a bath. What's shocking—head-shaking, tear-jerking, face-drawing shocking—is that in all that time, none of the neighbors pitched in! Or borrowed Noah's blueprints and laid out arks of their own! Every vacant lot in the vicinity could have been turned into a shipyard. It could have been a town full of arks, a flotilla of repentance and grace, thanks be to God, praise be to his name. But it wasn't. It was a town with just one ark, thanks be to God, praise be to his name. But even a single ark, bobbing like a cork, is still divine mercy. One ark that takes weeks and months and years to build—in plain sight, mind you—is a wide welcome and a gracious invitation.

When the first raindrops smacked on the great vessel's deck, on the rooftops, and on the tops of heads, no one was entirely shocked. Incredulous, maybe, but not shocked. The forecast had been before them all along, and it had grown louder and louder in their midst, plank by plank by plank.

When Noah entered the ark, he must have felt something like joy. Not joy at the loss of his neighbors, nor at the sinking of his hometown, nor at the washing away of the entire world, not even at his own vindication for belief and obedience. Noah entered the ark and felt joy to be with his God through the strange salvation his God provided.

Just as in the days of Noah, judgment is coming, and no one will be shocked. Incredulous once again, but not shocked. The forecast has been told in steeples and stained glass, on marquees on the church lawn, on billboards on the highway blazoned with Bible verses or theological zingers, in door-to-door evangelistic campaigns, and bumper stickers and ichthus auto decals, in sermons and Sunday School lessons, and cinematic retellings, by windy preachers wearing suits or skinny jeans. All these witnesses are like the ribs of a great ship reaching across the centuries and millennia.

Just as in the days of Noah, judgment will come unannounced -- as folks hustle off to all-you-can-eat buffets and wine tastings, destination weddings, divorce cruises, and Vegas remarriages.

Just as in the days of Noah, mercy will come with the storm.

Just as in the days of Noah, God will provide a holy escape.

Just as in the days of Noah, we will enter God's joyous presence through Jesus, our Ark.

Faith and practice: Why is it so distressing to us not to know the day or the hour? In what ways is not knowing the day and hour a grace?

DAY 7 – MATTHEW 24:36–44
In the Days of Noah, Part 2

When Noah entered the ark, he stepped simultaneously into salvation and loss. Salvation always brings loss. Salvation is a limitless gain received by leaving everything else behind. When the ark door closed, it closed its passengers into salvation, but it closed out the lives they had inhabited before.

Gone was the lone tree on the edge of his farm where he'd carved his initials along with his wife's in a jagged heart. Gone was the growth chart Noah had penciled on the door jamb of the utility closet. Gone were his neighbors, for whom he'd held out a longsuffering hope that they'd come to their senses and ask if he had room for one or two more aboard his unlikely ship. Gone were his past achievements, his plans unfulfilled, his dreams unrealized, and his commitments unaccomplished. Gone were opportunities missed, chances not taken, and regrets unreconciled. Everything that defined Noah, who he had been and still longed to be, was erased.

When did the weight of that loss wash over him? When the heavy door closed and shook the ark where it sat waiting in dry dock? While all within huddled in silence as the rain beat war drums on the ship's boards? Or when the ark first rocked and swayed as the waters lifted it from its keel blocks and set it adrift? Or maybe when he was below deck, mucking the stables, did think of home and miss it? Did he lean on the handle of his pitchfork, heaving with his own sobbing flood?

Salvation is always delivered in this shape. It is a leaving behind of everything we've belonged to and trusted in as we set out on a vast ocean of unknowing—with God as our tide and rudder. As the ark came together, Old Noah realized that he had already begun to say his goodbyes. With every nail, every peg, every crosscut, and every fitting, Noah was letting go of the only world he had known. And just like Noah, we must begin letting go. To rejoice in the return of Jesus, we must be willing to exit the world we have called home. How do you rejoice in something so fearful, so final?

This is usually where Christians try to hoodwink themselves into believing that they can shake the dust of this world from the soles of their shoes because there was never any good to be found here anyway. That is spiritual propaganda! We don't have to bully our souls to ready ourselves to leave this place. This place is filled with goodness, wonder, and beauty. Jesus gives us a short list: eating and drinking and marrying (24:38). Or we could think of these same gifts by the pleasures they gave: fullness, joy, and closeness. But these sustaining graces are choking curses if the God of love is not at the heart of them. Even if we use these things worshipfully, they still aren't the best expressions of God's love.

There is more! There is better! Somehow, there is waiting for us, *"exceedingly abundantly above all that we ask or think"* (Ephesians 3:20 NKJV). That is the secret to boarding the ark, to stepping from one world to the next. We leave this place with fondness and affection, sweet memories and tears, and we enter our eternal home with humility, trust, wonder, and more tears. Just as in the days of Noah, salvation feels like a cocktail of grief, loss, relief, and rejoicing all at once.

As the door of the ark was heaved shut, you can almost hear the rest of the vessel echo with an early whisper of Jesus's Gospel of coming away: *"Whoever would save his life will lose it, but whoever loses his life for my sake will find it"* (Matthew 16:26).

Faith and practice: What will you grieve most to leave behind from this world? What are you afraid to leave? What are you most eager to discover in the next world? Can you allow yourself to grieve and rejoice at the same time?

Week 2

GOD BRINGS US THROUGH CONFLICT INTO THE KINGDOM IN HIS SON

Isaiah 11:1–10; Romans 15:4–13; Matthew 3:1–12; Psalm 72:1–7, 18–19

DAY 8 – ISAIAH 11:1–10
The Shoot Is Greater Than the Stump

When God's salvation arrived, he wasn't much to look at. He's hardly what you'd build a kingdom out of, if given a choice. He was a shoot. A sprout. A sapling.

Now Jesse's son, David—there was a strong oak of a man, a savior-king if ever there was one. And yet, he did not accomplish salvation. By the end of his life, David needed salvation as much as anyone else. And David's glorious, supposedly saving reign was cut off. The oak was made into a stump.

But from the stump grows a sapling. One who resembles but surpasses. Not one who looks like a dream and ends with a fizzle, but one who looks like a disappointment and ends with a victory parade. From David's line, Jesus appears, and out of him, God grows fruit. The tree is gone, but the branch produces a harvest!

That is the mystery. The kingdom of salvation and grace don't usually look the way we want. We want them to look triumphant, impressive, strong, superior, muscular, and dominant. We want something pre-stump-like. But what God has chosen and sent looks insignificant, fragile, unimpressive, and even weak.

Why does God wrap his saving work in paradox and mystery? Why does he hide his grace so it can only be seen with eyes of faith? It is his unforgeable signature. He provides salvation that can't be duplicated, counterfeited, imitated, or mistaken.

From a cross of rejection, God raises a crop of fruitfulness. The foolish cross is God's wisdom. The guilty verdict is our innocence. The offense of the cross is our good standing. The scandal of the cross is our holy reputation. Where the tree was unable, the shoot is all-surpassing. It is nothing short of divine comedy that God would choose to create abundance from so little.

There is one final mystery seedling planted on Earth until Christ's return—the church. Not very impressive. Not entirely convincing. Not at all important. By all accounts, the church can be extremely ordinary, painfully dusty and antiquated, or awkwardly glitzy and relevant. Sometimes it is unrepentantly hypocritical. But this little stem is chosen and planted. You must look at it with eyes of faith, or you'll miss it. You'll have to look past the membership counts, the annual budget, the megaplex auditoriums, the steepled narthexes, the multiplied ministries, the livestream views, or the bestseller lists. All of that is old, oaken behavior.

Instead, look for the church to wear the mark of the kingdom on its heart. Look for the Spirit of the Lord resting and dwelling there (11:2). The presence of the Spirit is unmistakable. It looks like the church taking up the cause of the poor instead of its own comfort (11:4). It looks like giving equity to less-thans and outcasts (11:4). It looks like speaking the words of Jesus with belief and boldness, as if they bring world powers to their knees, and make predators cower (11:4). It looks like shedding every fleshly boast within reach in favor of wearing the meekness of Jesus's own righteousness and faithfulness (11:5). The church breathing deeply the Spirit of the Lord and acting like the kingdom produces the miracle of fruit from a ridiculous-looking stalk that couldn't produce so much as a leaf or blade on its own.

Only the Holy One can perform this final, spectacular feat. He will create something grand from something far less; he will send Jesus to kiss the mustard-seed faith of the kingdom and bring the church age to a glorious close.

Faith and practice: Rejoice in the mystery of the kingdom entrusted to the church. Rejoice that the power for reconciliation, renewal, and recreation comes from Jesus alone, and all the glory and celebration must be given to him.

DAY 9 – ISAIAH 11:1–10
New Eden

The branch of salvation is planted in the ruins of human effort, and it grows a harvest of what is most scarce in our world: peace. But this is not the flimsy, dented, paint-chipped knockoffs we try to pass for peace. It is not a truce, a time out, or a slab-footed dance around our unresolved conflicts. And it is certainly not that nonsense we are so fond of defaulting to: "Let's agree to disagree."

The branch in Isaiah's vision cultivates a peace that is dreamlike and otherworldly. It is unnatural peace, meaning no peace like this has been seen on the earth since the first two chapters of Genesis. In the world Isaiah dreams of, the wolf and the lamb are roommates (11:6). Apex predators have gone vegan (11:7). Hunters babysit their prey with the care they'd lavish on their own cubs (11:6). Toddlers play with knots of vipers (11:8), then waddle off to lead the whole menagerie on parade (11:6). These verses should read like a crime scene in the wild or an accident at the zoo, but they read like a paradise. The branch of salvation has landscaped from himself a New Eden.

But this passage can't simply be about the jungle-turned-nursery or wild-beasts-turned-neighbors. There was no law of the jungle before sin vandalized the purity and innocence of the garden. Everything in Isaiah's prophet-dream must point to a deeper shake-up. "In that day…" Isaiah writes, foreseeing a redemptive re-creation, a reconciled eternity (11:10). What he can't see is how Yahweh will replace genetic hostilities with healing. But we can see the full wonder of it. The rest of Scripture finishes painting the landscape that Isaiah began.

The agony of the cross is God's final, ferocious lunge at sin. The giddiness of the emptied tomb is death rendered bite-less, unable to clamp down on throats. In his sacrifice and glory, Jesus now stands as the author of a new law of nature where predators and prey are playmates.

It's a complete disruption of the old order:

Republicans and Democrats will trade compliments.
Pornographers and prudes will finally see clear-eyed.
Sluggards and overachievers will rest in the works of the faithful Son.
Alcoholics and teetotalers will drink the cup of the holy Groom.
Warmongers and peaceniks will find true security in the Lion who is the Lamb.
Socialists and capitalists will count the riches of Jesus.
Misogynists, feminists, segregationists, civil rights activists, the young and reckless, the old and curmudgeonly will size up themselves and each other in the perfections of Christ.

If some of these groups seem not to belong with the others, it is no more absurd to list them together than to believe that a leopard could play with a preschooler and leave him without a scratch. But that is the very thing promised. By God's grace, those who previously devoured each other will lose the taste for blood.

In the meantime, we show our eagerness for the return of Jesus by laying down our nursed hostilities and stepping over them into an illogical peace with others. Nothing could be more Gospel-shaped. When Jesus said to the crowd on the hillside one warm and dusty afternoon, *"Blessed are the peacemakers, for they shall be called the children of God,"* he wasn't joking (Matthew 5:9 KJV).

Faith and practice: The New Eden is a picture of unnatural peace established and won by the Gospel of Jesus Christ. If you were to begin to live as a preview of New Eden, however faintly and dimly, what unnatural peace would you display? What kinds of people (you know, *those* people) would Jesus call you to extend peace to? (And by peace, we do not mean coming to some kind of agreement. Leave "agreement" out of it. We mean what Isaiah means—relinquishing all claim to hostility.)

DAY 10 – ROMANS 15:4–13
Welcome

When Paul made the itinerant rounds to the churches he planted throughout his travels, he didn't just stay a spell; he practically moved in. He imposed. In doing so, he taught the theological meaning of welcome. *"Therefore, welcome one another as Christ has welcomed you,"* Paul writes to the Romans (15:7). In that one line, Paul dismisses all our Sunday morning versions of welcome as coordinated fakery. A smiley extrovert in the lobby handing out bulletins, a chirpy host behind a counter in the foyer pointing the way to kids' church, and a half-smile with a quick handshake during the passing of the peace—none of these even well-meaning gestures can measure up to the welcome Christ rolled out for us.

Our churches should do all these things, of course, but we shouldn't confuse them as welcome. They are more on the order of atmosphere, tone, or pre-welcome. They are customer service. They are important but aren't the deep welcome we should pursue. For that, verse 7 wants something vastly more from us—the welcome of Jesus himself.

All of God's activity in the world is a grand show of welcome—overcoming chaos with creation, overcoming offense with the cross, overcoming death with resurrection, and overcoming unbelief with faith. All these activities are the strong movement toward the welcome of Christ.

In fact, the whole Bible is one long story of welcome:
Adam and Eve, who were evicted from the garden and barred from eating the tree of life in their fallenness;
Noah, in his absurd lifeboat;
Abraham, a dried branch of a man who couldn't produce an heir but was promised a family tree as full as the twinkling star clusters overhead;
Sarah, who tried her best but couldn't keep from laughing when three

strangers turned up and told her to get the nursery ready;

Jacob, the promise-stealer who was bestowed with a rolling limp as a sacrament to show that he could lean on God to give blessings instead of trying to swindle them on his own;

Moses, who told the people to smear blood on their doorposts and follow him through a canyon of sea waters;

Rahab, the wrong sort of woman, whose name was written with capital letters into the royal lineage;

David, the shepherd boy and giant-killer, but no one's first choice for king;

Zechariah, the ragged priest, the most holy in all the land and still filthy as a latrine;

Mary, who received a string of "blessed-are-yous" to hold her steady in faith against the whispers and rumors that floated through the village as her belly grew;

Peter, the shaky rock;

The women who went to the tomb before dawn and ran all the way back—women, who were not considered credible witnesses of anything, but who were shown the resurrection first;

Thomas, who said, "I'll believe it when I see it," and then the risen Jesus walked through the locked door and invited Thomas to touch his wounds so there could be no doubt;

Paul, mastermind of massacres who became a tent-revivalist;

The circumcised who were not saved by their surgery but by the faith it awakened in their hearts; and the uncircumcised, too, who didn't count at all until they were received into the family of twinkling stars promised to Abraham as children;

And you. And me. The Gospel is the same story of radical welcome played out over and over again.

This story should change the way we ponder and practice welcome. Welcome is not just social etiquette. Welcome is an unconditional embrace—to be part of something, fully, enthusiastically, and without reservation. In the final welcome, all distance will be erased. The final welcome is whispered louder and louder in every true welcome we extend, and in every true welcome we accept.

Faith and practice: The people you are hesitant and anxious to accept are probably the very people you should. You will have more of the wild joy of Christ if you do.

DAY 11 – MATTHEW 3:1–12
Baptized

Baptism is an escape from judgment by way of salvation, and the Old Testament is filled with strange versions of baptism:

Noah's ark sloshing over the top of the raging waves;
Blood painted on door frames in Egypt;
Salt spray from the Red Sea, cut into a watery gorge;
Rahab's red cord, tied from her window in the city wall;
The blazing fire that preserved Daniel in the sight of his enemies,
And the lion pit that saved him a second time to show the persistent power of his God.

In the New Testament, this same view of baptism is consolidated in John, the prophet of the wilds, waist-deep in the Jordan River, pouring water over all sinners who know they need saving. Somehow, in ways that words can't quite capture, they sense that this repentance, this turning in water, marks a participation, an inclusion in the salvation that will carry God's people out of judgment—like Noah, Moses, Rahab, and Daniel. So one by one, they climb, dripping and grinning, up the muddy bank as another penitent sinner splashes into the river.

To the surprise of absolutely no one, the religious leaders have wandered out to the sticks in search of John the Baptizer and his sodden pilgrims. Anytime there is a religious ceremony or a tent revival, the Pharisees and Sadducees turn up to vet the event. In part, they turn up out of jealousy, asking, "What's John got that we haven't?" In part, they know an opportunity when they smell one—people searching for spiritual comfort and assurance are sectarians and rigorists in the making. In part, they come as a precaution, "just in case," to ensure all their bases are covered. Finally, they come to watch John's baptism so no one can accuse them of leaving even a single observance unobserved.

And when the Pharisees and Sadducees show up, they stand on the bank, dripping more with skepticism and scorn than with the waters of grace and hope. John pounces on the moment and calls out to them as he receives another candidate for baptism down in the river. He rebukes them, saying that if their hearts aren't in this washing, they may as well go drown themselves in a pit of moral filth.

Then John leans into the theology of baptism. This moment is a picture. This is a token, a signifier. This is a spiritually alive enactment of what is to come, the real baptism. Everyone will be baptized, but not everyone will be baptized in the same way.

John says that judgment and salvation come in tandem—some will be washed, and some will be washed away. His words match what Jesus says of his own baptism. For Jesus, baptism is not a reference to John's water but the looming judgment of the cross (see Mark 10:38; Luke 12:49).

Later, Paul pushes it one step further when he says that we were baptized into Christ. We were included in his crucifixion, but our participation was beam-less and nail-less. For believers, baptism celebrates that we get all the satisfaction of Christ's cross-shaped judgment and none of the agony and torment. For believers, baptism illustrates that Christ has passed through our judgment and we have been spared. We have been kissed by fire but not consumed. We have come out dripping but not drowned. According to John, baptism means that as the Holy Spirit passes over the earth, some of us come alive, and some of us become hardened. And John doesn't explain any further than that, probably because he can't! Even prophets have limited insight, and so do we. We can't understand the mystery of the separation of wheat from chaff (Matthew 3:12). We can't wring our hands, clench our fists, or grind our teeth. Well, we can—but it changes nothing. Some of us have passed through. Some of us once were all chaff and stalk, but the Spirit blew through us and transformed us into wheat.

Now the only thing to do is take our places to meet Jesus when he returns for the final baptism. We will not be found on the bank with the Pharisees and Sadducees—scowling, arms crossed, harrumphing as we judge the coming judgment. We will stand, dripping and smiling with the crowds, with the needy who know it, with the other stones turned children of Abraham, vipers made disciples, dead stumps become orchards in bloom. We will stand charred, smiling, and saved.

Faith and practice: Can you think of a waterless "baptism" you have received as a reassertion of divine grace, a passing through judgment and not being lost?

Does this way of talking about baptism change how you will celebrate the next baptism you witness? What will be different?

DAY 12 – MATTHEW 3:1–12
Axe and Fork

John the Baptist would be a terrible addition to our nativity sets. While the shepherds, magi, and parents crowd around the manger, John would be the figurine standing away from the crèche, frozen in a plastic scream, with an axe in one hand and a pitchfork in the other. Nothing like a little fire and brimstone to spoil the holiday spirit.

John the Baptist doesn't seem to fit the Advent season, yet he's its most prominent figure. Oddly enough, he shows up in the Advent readings more than anyone else. And John's appearances disregard chronology! During Advent, he doesn't show up as the fetus jumping in Elizabeth's womb. No, what we get during our Advent readings is the full-grown John, mad prophet of the desert, all broody in his camel hair shirt and belt, foraging for bugs and honey and sleeping in the scrub brush by the river.

But what if we've misjudged John? John makes a sharp critique of the Pharisees and Sadducees, calling them a ball of snakes (which they had coming, by the way). He issues a warning about the axe of judgment sizing up the roots of fruitless trees, another warning about the winnowing fork ready to clear away wheatless stalks, and another warning of a bonfire made from the aforementioned chopped trees and winnowed stalks. With all these warnings, John is pegged. For the rest of Christian history, John is typecast as a sermonic firebreather and misanthrope telling crowds of pilgrims that they need to repent and be washed before judgment can fall on them.

That hardly seems fair. John came preaching that the kingdom of heaven had arrived, and judgment and grace had come with it. Judgment always accompanies grace, but when we hear of the two together, we only hear the one. Judgment always seems to eclipse grace for readers and hearers.

Judgment always seems to cancel grace out. In truth, however, judgment is part of grace—right down to the chopping axe, the winnowing fork, and the burning fire.

Every farmer knows that before you can enjoy a grove of thriving trees, the barren ones must be removed. Every reaper knows that before the harvest is gathered into the barn, the husks, shells, and stems must be swept away. The fields and the granary floors must be cleared. When Jesus returns, he will bring his kingdom in full. Judgment clears the ground for the arrival of full redemption. Judgment makes room for complete reconciliation. Judgment opens the way for perfect shalom to fill up the space. The preview of this judgment is the threshing of the cross to clear our hearts of sin, guilt, and shame—making room for an abundance of new growth in the resurrection.

Still, this text seems to speak harshly, through clenched teeth and hissing breath. John's warnings cause readers to glisten with nervous perspiration. But John assures us that the one who raises the axe and pitches the fork is the master gardener (Matthew 3:12). John continually holds out to the dripping crowds and sweaty readers alike the good news of repentance! Repentance is the miracle that occurs when the Holy Spirit causes the tree and the stalk to realize that they do not grow fruit for themselves. The crop is not for the plant. Repentance is the supernatural resolve to devote, dedicate, and donate more of ourselves to the kingdom of Jesus and resist every rival kingdom, no matter how shallow or sophisticated. Repentance is the electric awakening that sees God's re-creation in the world manifested in Jesus alone, and repentance desires to have the power and presence of Jesus publicly manifested across our lives. Repentance keeps the axe from swinging, the fork from plunging, and the weed piles from burning. Repentance is another way to make room. And the kingdom, or fruit, fills the space.

Maybe it's not such a bad idea to have John the Baptist figurines in our nativity sets after all. He doesn't fit chronologically, but he sure fits theologically. He's a reminder at the very least that the kingdom, established on earth through the baby Jesus, doesn't fit easily into our routines. Just like any newborn, the kingdom takes up our entire lives. You wouldn't quite know it to look at him, but this little baby is sent to make us axe- and fork-proof. He is sent to make bare trees and empty stalks a windfall.

Faith and practice: Repentance never stops. See if you can sense how the Holy Spirit moves you to make more room in your life for the kingdom.

DAY 13 – ROMANS 15:4–13
Abounding

Theologically speaking, hope is a firmly rooted confidence in someone else. It is not a wish assigned to a coin and tossed in a fountain, a dream lassoed to a shooting star, or a desire huffed out with birthday candles.

It's also not a certainty. Hope doesn't know precisely how everything is going to work out. We can't sign off on it or renegotiate the terms. Hope is different. Hope relies on someone else to come through in a pinch—without pacing, hand-wringing, or breaking a sweat. Hope is the feeling of rocking back in your chair, arms behind your head, smiling like the cat who ate the canary. Our confidence is not in the plan because we often can't see the plan being worked out as it unfolds around us. Our confidence is in God, who brings all things about for his glory and our good, as infuriating and confounding as our circumstances may be (Romans 8:28). Hope is the conviction, "His love will come through. It always does."

The bulk of this passage seems to be a strange argument about Gentiles and Jews. These mentions usually signal a debate over who's in and who's out, and this is no exception. Paul says that Jesus was circumcised to show he was the one whom Yahweh promised to the patriarchs, and then he quotes four different Old Testament prophecies that make room for the Gentiles in God's favor through Jesus, too. If you are circumcised, God kept his promises by sending Jesus, and if you are uncircumcised, God has brought you in as if you were part of the promise all along.

Hope is what allows you to rejoice in Christ's salvation if you are a Gentile and what allows you to rejoice over Gentiles if you are a Jew. It's this simple. Where the rest of the world demands a judicial inquiry, hope celebrates with balloons and hats and noisemakers and confetti. A naked figure droops from a cross, and the guilty no longer hang their heads in shame; a tomb with a broken-down door moves people to dance on their grave plots like they know something their neighbors don't; and Gentiles (Gentiles!) run through the church without all that feverish, competitive law-keeping! Just like that, outsiders are in! This is hope.

Paul has soaked this little block of verses with his understanding of hope. He starts by saying that the whole Bible was written to make sure we never run low on hope (Romans 15:4). At the end, Paul says we are supposed to abound in it (15:13). That's like saying we're to put ourselves on a strict diet of the stuff. Along the way, he points out that hope comes from God, and it is supernatural (15:13). It is ours to flex and push to its limits in the power of the Holy Spirit. This is good news for missionary exiles.

In hope, we continue to love and serve our neighbors and proclaim the love and grace of Jesus, not worried about their reactions. In hope, we live like the re-creation has already started, even when no one else can see it. In hope, we stretch our arms over the landscape and say, "It doesn't look like it, but the Gospel is winning here!" In hope, we watch the skies, squint past the clouds, and whisper to ourselves, "Maybe today."

The wonder of redemptive hope is like being brought to a movie theater for a grand premiere. After we settle into our seats with popcorn, sodas, and candy, the house lights go down, and the screen flickers to life. We're engrossed in the start, followed by a few jump cuts to scenes that pull us along the plot. Then there is a jagged edit and a sudden splice to the very end. We are shown the end! It is less film and more spoiler! The house lights come up, and a producer, who looks an awful lot like the apostle Paul, steps down front to announce, "You'll know the middle bits as they happen, as you live them. But you can count on the end." And the audience sends up a tremendous cheer as we launch the remnants of our popcorn buckets into the air and walk out, arm-in-arm, blinking into the sunlight, abounding in hope.

Faith and practice: What has been your understanding of hope up to now? Wishful thinking? A demand for certainty? Or Paul's version? Can you imagine yourself not stumbling into hope from time to time, but abounding in it?

DAY 14 - PSALM 72:1–7, 18–19
One-and-Only King

According to the postscript (Psalm 72:20), this is David's last musical prayer, and he sings it for Solomon (72:1). Who better to pray for the one who rises to the throne than the one who sat there before him?

In a way, there is nothing unusual about David's prayer. It is one of nine Royal Psalms that herald the sitting king of Israel as God's king. Israel's king was supposed to be an earthly extension of God's heavenly rule. So, it's the usual and expected prayer of blessing for God's king on earth as he does God's bidding from heaven.

Psalm 72 is loaded with all the typical royal hyperbole and exaggeration: may he rule forever, may the kings of the earth bow down before him, may he dispense perfect justice as the daily order of his court, and so on. It's easy for us to yawn through this psalm, to feel disconnected from the promise. It's all the usual kingly bluster that somehow never reaches the people. You can imagine a worshiper in the Temple, some years after David composed the psalm, attending dutifully with the congregation but singing through clenched teeth, "Yes, yes, justice and righteousness and peace, but where are they, O king?! And yes, live forever, longer than the sun and the moon. It would be just our luck. And may the just flourish, but probably not, because everyone knows it's the kings who flourish on the backs of the people...."

But wait. We can remember that David, Israel's second king, is writing this psalm with Solomon his successor on his mind and heart. And here's the difference: he writes it at the end! At the end! That makes all the difference. If David had written the psalm at the start of his reign, it would have read like the idealistic overpromising of a politician on the campaign trail. It's easy to roll our eyes and close our ears because rhetoric is not policy. But David writes this psalm, his last psalm, at the end of his reign, which is to say, at the end of his life! What if it's not a boast, not kingly idealism? What if it's a confession?

David is using the form of the Royal Psalms, but you can almost hear him pleading underneath, "This is the king the people long for, the king you long for them to have, the king I aspired to and so desperately wanted to be. Now bless and keep Solomon, "because who on earth can be king in your name and after your character, O Lord?" The answer to David's cry comes in verses 18 and 19: "Every earthly king will be a disappointment, but God's heavenly King will not."

The ache of the psalm is answered in Jesus. In fact, if the psalm has done its job, it will have made us very picky about our kings. Not just any old king will do. We want a one-and-only king. We want a king who judges, rules, decrees, conquers, and reigns from under the beams of a used-up cross and from the doorway of a broken tomb. We want a king who lifts up the lowly and presses down the oppressors (72:4), a king whose generosity washes through us and washes over our neighbors (72:6), whose blessings are so full and so free that we are desperate to give them away. We want precisely this king because God has promised him in the psalm. Jesus is the only King who can wear this psalm without hyperbole! It is tailor-made for him.

If the ache of the psalm is answered in Jesus, then the ache of our hearts and bodies for finished redemption and completed shalom can only be answered in his return. If David's response to the wounds of human brokenness was to pray for the arrival of a better king, maybe we should do the same. *"Amen. Come, Lord Jesus"* (Revelation 22:20).

Faith and practice: Pray through Psalm 72, especially verses 1–7. As you do, praise God for Jesus, the returning Redeemer, as the fulfillment of the verses. The Lord Jesus was a fulfillment David couldn't see, but we can.

Notes

Week 3

GOD BRINGS US THROUGH EXILE TOWARD HOME THROUGH HIS SON

Isaiah 35:1–10; James 5:7–10; Matthew 11:2–11; Psalm 146:1–10

DAY 15 – ISAIAH 35:1–10
Fools' Highway

Salvation is always dramatic. It comes on the current of judgment and overturns the status quo. It is an overcoming, a reversal.

From barren to lush.
From sobs to songs.
From hopelessness to hallelujahs.
From exile to exodus.

Isaiah 35 is the good news that God brings his people joyfully out of the judgment of exile. Israel has been sacked and carried off into captivity by Babylon for the sin of idolatry. Idolatry is hard to conceive in the modern world, but instead of getting hung up on statues and sculptures, imagine idolatry as all our distorted cravings worn externally. We aren't prone to figurines the way the ancients were, but our fears and warped desires are enshrined as pursuits, ambitions, and drives. Idolatry in our age may look different in expression, but it is unchanged in essence. Idolatry is a spiritual misalignment that manifests in a physical captivity.

But Yahweh, in his mercy, sometimes allows us to be captured by our idols. In mercy, he lets us feel their emptiness and languish under their false promises. Even exile is a grace in the hand of God because the pain of exile turns to renewed dependence and hope. Out of the bad news of exile comes the good news that we can't bear to be without our true Savior. But Jesus paid for our every idolatry. He carried them up the hill to Calvary and felt their weight on the cross. But he breezed past them as he walked victoriously out of the tomb. By faith, we can walk away from our voluntary captivities just that easily.

In Isaiah 35, we have another picture of this reality, as the Savior God promises to save Israel from exile and lead them all the way home with a parade of reversal.

Ruins will be rebuilt.
Overgrown wilds will become farm plots again.
The desert will blossom in joy and song (35:1–2).
The burning sand seas will flow with streams (35:7).
And the ghost towns where jackals have moved in will be cul-de-sacs and boulevards (35:7).

Salvation is always the story of drastic reversals, from home to wasteland to home again. So it's fitting that the road of reversal is a highway (35:8). Isaiah loves a good highway. What's behind the prophet's obsession? A highway is a straight line, an unobstructed path into the redeeming presence of the Lord. There are no steep climbs and treacherous descents. The journey is not difficult, and it is safe. There are no bends, no blind curves or corners, no hiding spots for bandit ambushes, and no places for lions or predators to lurk and hunt. In fact, there are no lions here at all (35:9)! There are no stalkers, no enemies. This highway, the way of holiness, is impassable to the unclean who revel in their uncleanness, but to the repentant, those alive by faith, the road is straight, flat, and open. And here's the most astounding reversal of the whole lot—this highway is so clear, so wide-open and easy, a fool can travel it and not get lost (35:8)!

For now, we wait in exile. We are in a hostile land. This is a wasteland of faith and a desert of counterfeit righteousness and false gospels. Beasts roam here, and hunters prowl for our hearts and bodies. But we long for reversal and home. When Jesus returns, when we least expect him, he is our great reversal. He is our highway. His salvation is so generous and comical it makes even the fool a sage. Let every fool rejoice!

> **and practice:** What reversals have you experienced as an outpouring of God's grace? Do you regularly celebrate and marvel at your reversals, or have trouble remembering them? Do you crowd them out with complaints? Your faith-filled reversals will give you a glimpse of the great reversal. Use them as deposits of hope and confidence while in exile.

DAY 16 – ISAIAH 35:1–10
Anatomy of Hope

Despair is worn in our bodies. When Isaiah describes Israel in the captivity of exile (Isaiah 35:3–6), he isn't suggesting that the people have all been struck blind, deaf, mute, and invalid. He is describing their emotional and spiritual health. In their souls and bodies, they carry the sorrow of sin and the grief of God. Their state matches what Isaiah was told during his commissioning:

"Go, and say to this people: 'Keep on hearing, but do not understand; keep on seeing, but do not perceive.' Make the heart of this people dull, and their ears heavy, and blind their eyes" (Isaiah 6:9).

Faith and unbelief are psychosomatic. This makes sense because we are whole beings, complete creatures. We are not a ramshackle assemblage of disconnected parts. We are fallen, but we are not partial. Worship requires body and soul striving together. So does sin.

Isaiah acknowledges the consuming sorrow of the people (Isaiah 35:3–6):
>Their hands are listless and idle.
>Their knees can't hold them upright.
>Their eyes are milky with spiritual cataracts.
>Their ears are muted and ringing.
>They open their silent mouths and gape like fish in the bottom of a boat.
>Their ankles and feet have nowhere to carry them.
>Their hearts are a tangle of fear and anxiety.

Until God comes and saves them (35:4).
Then:
A kaleidoscope of color, a Pantone wheel.
Music, like laughter and crying all at once. Like a favorite song er grows tired and overplayed.

WEEK 3

Hands that are swift, nimble, lithe, and calloused with the work of love.
Knees that are sturdy and walk undeterred and undistracted toward the presence of God.
Tongues that belt out their joy like Pavarotti.
Feet and ankles that jig and reel and stomp with the good news, kicking the furniture out of the way and pulling the enfeebled out of their seats.
Hearts that are bold, not faint, declaring: "Be strong; fear not! Be strong; fear not! Be strong; fear not!"

If sorrow and despair are psychosomatic, then so are hope and rejoicing. If sorrow and despair show up in our bodies, then hope and joy have tissue and bone and muscle, too.

Advent means making room for both. We are still in exile. We sing it in our carols, "O come, O come Emmanuel, and ransom captive Israel." But we are also sure that our exile is coming to a divine end and our full redemption is near. The cross is silent, the tomb is open and empty, and Jesus stands at the door, poised to walk through one last time. The emotional complexity of Advent for whole beings is like wearing mismatched clothes—sackcloth and ashes, torn robes with party hats, and black armbands with evening gowns. Advent is the answer to our half-dressed neighbors, the doomsayers, and the Pollyanna optimists. The people of Christ wear the story of salvation in our bodies; we are in continuous mourning interrupted by fits of inconsolable joy.

When Jesus comes, we will swap our bodies of sorrow and hope for bodies of glory.

Faith and practice: Which do you do more: mourn or rejoice? Chances are you favor one. Which do you need to add to your daily practice, worship, and waiting? Which will make your Advent experience fuller?

DAY 17 – JAMES 5:7–10
Patient as Prophets

"Wait like a prophet," James advises. "Be patient as prophets" (James 5:10). This is a strange thing to say because prophets aren't known for their saintly patience. Elisha called two sow bears out of the woods to feast on forty-two juvenile delinquents who pointed and laughed because Elisha had grown a little thin on top (2 Kings 2:23–25). Not thrilled with his new assignment, Jonah went AWOL until Yahweh dispatched creation to bring him in. Hosea stormed brothels, flinging back curtains and kicking down doors in search of his promiscuous wife. Jeremiah held a clay pot overhead and called, "Wait till Yahweh gets his hands on you, Israel!" before smashing it to smithereens (Jeremiah 19:11). The saints weren't quite the role models of forbearance we like to think they were.

But when it came to suffering, no one could outdo the prophets. They faced jeering crowds, angry mobs, wanted posters, abusive punches, and fast-pitched rocks. They were dumped down a well, tossed overboard in a maritime squall, and swallowed whole in a whale belly. Prophets were not admired, envied, or welcomed when they came into town.

But the prophets' job description was straightforward enough. The prophet speaks in the name of the Lord. The prophet bears the message of God, and the salary is mistreatment (James 5:10). People don't want to hear about judgment, and they certainly don't want to hear that judgment is coming for them. People don't want to be told to repent. People are defiant when confession and contrition are called for. For any prophet wearing a sandwich board on a street corner during lunch hour yelling that the end is near, but grace is nearer still, it's like talking to the dirt. "But!" points out James in verse 7, "Sometimes the dirt receives a seed, and that seed sprouts, and goes to leaf, and throws fruit."

In most cases, the prophet won't know if the message will be received, just like the farmer can't know if the seed will sprout. What happens with the seed after the sowing is neither the farmer's work nor the prophet's. Sometimes fruit comes early, sometimes late, and sometimes thistles, brambles, and nettles grow instead. Most of the time, the fruiting crop and the stinging weeds grow together, side by side. Farmers and prophets do virtually the same work, just in different kinds of soil.

The only thing the prophet can know is the message, and it is usually in the delivery that the prophet's temper flares. But the results of the message always call for patience and often bring suffering. During this long season of Advent, from the ascension of Jesus until now, you too are prophets—mini-prophets perhaps, prophets with a lowercase "p," but prophets, nonetheless. You have a message to speak:

Jesus came to bring redemption.
Jesus will return to complete redemption. You can bet your life on it.
Jesus appeared in holy flesh to be crucified, to rise, and to ascend. He did not do all of this to leave the work half-done. He will return to make you holy flesh, too—and anyone who repents and believes. Anyone.

The bad news for prophets is that they usually end up in a whale belly or a half-dry well somewhere along the way. The good news is that this treatment makes the job and message even more urgent.

Faith and practice: Have you ever noticed how you suffer for the Gospel? (You've probably never thought of it, but you do.) How is suffering for the Gospel a blessing and a gift instead of punishment and discipline? If you can see the beauty and glory in patient proclamation, you will be a dangerous "prophet" while you wait for Jesus to return.

DAY 18 – JAMES 5:7–10
Native Tongue

Grumbling is the noise we make while we wait: the DMV, traffic jam, ticket counter, security checkpoint, and customer service. We tell ourselves that grumbling is the language of inconvenience, but in truth, it is the language of fear. It expresses the strong suspicion that we are being mishandled, overlooked, forgotten, and left to fend for ourselves in the face of some perceived injustice.

In these few verses, James tries to flip our assumption that grumbling is natural. Instead, he suggests that it is invasive and pestilent. James's first move is to assert that waiting is not mistreatment. By using the farm imagery of planting, James proclaims that waiting is about germination. Yahweh does not give you seasons of waiting to toy with you or to exasperate you. He gives you waiting so you will grow—in faith, trust, perseverance, hope, wisdom, beauty, kindness, generosity, grace, love, and every attribute of godliness we could list until there were no more paper or ink to list them. In other words, all our waiting is given to us to increase his likeness in us, resemblance to the God who saved us by adopting us as his children.

Why so long a wait between our expulsion from the garden and the first advent of Jesus? To allow millennia of clinging to messianic promise to build an all-out thirst for his arrival.

Why so long, some thirty years, for his epiphany and self-revelation? To rearrange our kingdom expectations.

Why so long between the black skies of Golgotha and the sunburst morning of the broken tomb? To feel the greedy clamp of death and to feel the stronger command for death to relent, release, open, and turn loose.

Why so long a wait for the return of Christ? To make us hungry for re-creation, and to give us the role of walking the earth as its rejoicing foreshocks.

But when all this waiting is detached from growth, grumbling seeps in. In fact, in unreflective waiting, we make grumbling our first language. It has become our native tongue. It's nearly an anthem with us.

So James performs a nifty piece of theological jiu-jitsu. He warns us against grumbling as if it were the worst sin imaginable—cardinal, mortal, deadly. We tend to treat complaining like childishness or immaturity, a deficit of character at most. But James says it is a judgeable offense (5:9)! Grumbling is what we do when we lack patience in suffering. Grumbling is what we do to fill up the space of absent faith. Then, James dials in a sharper focus on the offense—do not grumble against your brothers and sisters. The language of brothers and sisters is not grumbling and fighting. If we are remade, refashioned in the cross and resurrection, then as brothers and sisters speak the ridiculous language of love. If Christ has accomplished all to give you all, if no bad behavior or treatment can diminish your Christly inheritance, then you are free to love in the name of Jesus without initiation and regardless of return!

Finally, James throws out this doozy of a warning: *"Do not grumble against one another, brothers, so that you may not be judged,"* followed by the quizzical, *"the Judge is standing at the door"* (5:9).

But what if!? What if the mention of the judge at the door is a clue to the nature of the judgment? What if the judgment described here is not only the judge bursting through to find us treating one another as enemies and torments instead of saints and holy siblings? What if the judgment is a delay of the thing we need and long for most? What if the judge holds off walking in? What if this postponement is to give us more time to learn a new native language—the language we should have been fluent in long before now? Like patience, faith, and love toward each other?

Just like the farmer, James seems to suggest that Jesus is waiting for the planted seed to grow. The good news for us is that, once again, even our suffering is a mysterious grace.

Faith and practice: To prompt your reflection, get a piece of paper and keep count of how many times you grumble. You can itemize it, listing the occasion and the content of your grumbling, or you can just make tally marks on the paper. Your emotions at the final number may vary—but above all, you can repent, rejoice, and ask for renewal. Then, consider how you can speak the Gospel to yourself in place of each grumbling. You could write out what you wish you had said in each case. You could go into an empty room and speak your alternatives out loud. You could pray. Maybe sing a song of faith. To learn a new language, you must practice. You must use new words in place of the old.

DAY 19 - MATTHEW 11:2-11
Forerunner

"Are you sure you aren't leaving anything out? That's all he said?" John asked his disciples through the bars of jail. Bearing Jesus's reply to the baptizer, John's disciples cleared their throats, broke off from John's hot gaze, and shuffled their feet. They knew what John was hoping to hear, but it was achingly absent.

John had done his job, hadn't he? He'd poured water on the crowds and put the fear of God in them. He'd called the self-approving Pharisees a nest of snakes, as slithery and fork-tongued as the serpent draped through the tree limbs in the garden. He'd given the lecherous king a good finger-wagging, and in the royal courtroom, no less. And for it all, John was thrown in the clink. John knew this was the customary handling of prophets, but this time was different. The kingdom had come! Hadn't it? The kingdom was here! Wasn't it?

So John sent his disciples to Jesus for some answers. "Cousin, tell me you're the one. Cousin, tell me this isn't a put-on. Tell me, Cousin—I haven't made a terrible mistake or a terrible fool of myself?" John's a fool, alright, but not the kind he fears he is. He's a fool on the highway of grace, and Jesus says as much in reply.

"Decide for yourself, John. The blind have 20/20 vision, the lame are dancing in the streets, the lepers are handing out hugs, the deaf are chasing songbirds in the park, the dead are reselling their burial plots, and the poor believe their ship is about to come in (Matthew 11:4–5)." John would recognize this list of messianic signs as a combined inventory from Isaiah 35:5–6 and Isaiah 61:1. In the blurry overlap of all the marvelous things Jesus was reported to be doing on his preaching tour, which sounded remarkably like the wonders that would identify Messiah at his appearing, John was meant to find the answer he was looking for.

But still, there was one messianic sign left off the list: *"Liberty to the captives, and the opening of the prison to those who are bound"* (Isaiah 61:1).

Jesus left that part of the prophetic promise out. John turned from the bars, laid down on his pile of sour straw, and wept. Outside his cell, John's disciples slid their backs down the bars and joined their master, sobbing into arms folded across their knees.

But it wasn't just what Jesus left out; it's what he said out loud that was troublesome. As John's disciples returned with Jesus's answer, Jesus talked to the crowd, presumably hoping that this would get back to the prophet, too. "John is no reed shaking in the wind, so don't think for a minute that he'll buckle in prison! When you came out to him, what did you find? An influencer dressed in Versace silks and Gucci loafers? There is nothing soft about John! Every inch of him is fitted for the kingdom, which is good form because the kingdom of God is no weekend at the spa" (Matthew 11:7–14).

The most important statement for John, and all of us with him, is the one that stings most: *"Blessed is the one who is not offended by me"* (11:6). A better translation might be, "Happy, or blessed, is the one who is not scandalized by me." But John most certainly was scandalized by Jesus. His message to Jesus was scandal: "Why am I here?! You are planning a jailbreak, aren't you?!" And our cries are scandalized complaints, too. We may not all be waiting behind bars, but we have all been waiting a long time for the return of Jesus, and under duress. "Why are we still here?! You are coming back, aren't you?! How long do we have to carry on like this?!" Of course, Jesus is coming back—and soon, according to his promise (whatever soon means).

But before he sweeps unbelief and godlessness away eternally, Jesus must beat them. He must humiliate them. In other words, you can round up righteousness, holiness, truth, peace, love, faithfulness, and grace—you can lock them away, chain them to the dungeon wall, march them to the executioner's block, nail them to a cross, or seal them in a tomb—but you cannot force them to surrender. And in that scandal, we are healed.

John was not forgotten. He was the forerunner (11:10)! John was the first instance of Gospel triumph through suffering. John was not a casualty; he was the battlefield where the Gospel won its earliest victories, even in a dungeon and under an executioner's axe.

Maybe, when the quaking sobs turned John loose, the Gospel settled on him. Maybe the word forerunner echoed in his heart. The Gospel had not failed. John's ministry was not a cruel trick. Even behind bars, John was a confrontation of every sinful power, a living proclamation that the kingdom had come and was claiming a bigger and broader stake. Sitting in the corner of his jail, maybe John became freer than a child running through the Galilean hills. And maybe, right there in the cell block, John also became a forerunner of Paul—and started singing (Acts 16:25).

Faith and practice: Can you identify places where the Gospel may be winning in your life, even where it looks like it is not? Can you find places where you are a confrontation to brokenness and a proclamation of grace? Singing is a great help in the struggle—it reminds you that the fight isn't fair, your side is far stronger, and the joy of the Lord is your strength (Nehemiah 8:10).

DAY 20 – PSALM 146:1–10
The Forever King

Every king's legacy is the same in the end. Even the grandest of kings return to dust. But each one starts off with such promise, don't they? Believed to be God's representatives on earth, stars appeared in the sky to announce their birth, and stars fell out of the night when they died. When they passed through the streets in a royal procession, the people lined the way in a mad frenzy, "Long live the king!" and "O king, live forever!" And the people meant it, most of the time.

The health of the kingdom was tied to the demeanor of the king. A strong and beneficent king meant years of prosperity. A petty and cruel king lingered like a plague. The king is the kingdom, in other words. They rise and fall together.

But even the mightiest of kings would eventually fade. Their limbs would grow feeble. Their hair would turn gray. Their teeth would fall out, and the chef would serve less meat and more soup. The kingly stride would degrade to a slump and shuffle. Eventually, every king is reduced to an inky line on a scroll, a statue in a garden, or an ornate carving on the lid of a sarcophagus in a drafty cathedral. No king, no matter how great, can reach past the grave.

And so the psalmist whispers to us a piece of advice: "Do not trust in princes or rulers. They cannot save, though they all promise it" (Psalm 146:3). It's no surprise then, that when voters are interviewed at political rallies or protests—wearing t-shirts and hats with slogans, holding placards with a candidate's name or catchphrase, yelling into the microphone, and pointing at the camera—many of them are angry and outraged. They are anxious, fearful, scornful, insulted, insulting, hostile, hateful, bristling with violence, sulking in defeat, and often prophesying some national doom. The psalmist warned us, and we didn't heed his whisper. We trust princes and rulers to be our salvation, but God is still sovereign over their power. Said another way, if we trust too much in the kings and rulers of the earth, our salvation is not at stake, but our peace and joy are—and maybe our purpose and mission in this place as well.

The psalmist has a second whisper for us. "Do you want to be happy? Then make Yahweh your only source of help" (146:5). The psalmist never comes right out and calls Yahweh 'king' in the psalm, but when he compares him to the limits of mortal princes, he makes the point as clear as a royal standard snapping in the wind.

The entire reign of Yahweh is dedicated and devoted to our help. Modern ears miss the rhetorical shape of the argument, but it roughly follows this line of reasoning. God made the spheres—heaven, earth, and seas—and he makes himself the faithful keeper of all that is in them (146:6). Unlike the kings of the earth, God is so faithful that he looks to the unimpressive, the overlooked, and the discarded—and he rules with them in mind: the oppressed and hungry, the prisoner, the blind, the burdened, the refugee, the widow, and the orphan (146:6-8). God loves us in our vulnerability, need, and frailty. He is a God determined to be our help!

Why else would this forever King enthrone himself on a cross under the weight of our expansive guilt? Why else would he hold court in the laughing echo of an open tomb? Why else would he spread his rule by pouring his Spirit over the world instead of marching armies across it? Why else would he delay his return for so long? Why else would he disappoint us with all the counterfeits and rival kings we invite to seduce and mislead our hearts—if not to make himself our only and true help? This King does not falter and does not fade (146:10).

Like all the other psalms in this section of the psalter, this one has a beautiful symmetry—it begins and ends the same way. There is another symmetry tucked inside it as well. This God spends his being on our help. Convinced of this, we spend our lives seeking and praising him for it.

Faith and practice: Where do you seek help other than the Father, Son, and Spirit? Have you found help apart from God? If so, did it cost you in other ways? What would you change in your daily spiritual practices to help you seek God more?

DAY 21 – PSALM 146:1–10
Jacob's God

From the womb, Jacob was a hustler. His name translates to "heel grabber," a nod to his first attempted swindle when he tried to nose past his older twin in the delivery room. It wouldn't be the only play he would make for the blessed rights of the firstborn. There was the time he strapped wool to his forearms and wore his brother's clothes to pay a disguised deathbed visit to his blind father. Then there was the time he met his dimwitted and ravenous sibling, just in from a hunt, with a pot of savory beans cooking over an open fire.

Jacob, the grabber, always had a trick up his sleeve. To shake his hand was to lose your wristwatch and rings. Even when he was outconned by his father-in-law, Laban, Jacob couldn't bring himself to go straight. In one last *coup d'état,* Jacob stole Laban's entire shrine full of idols and made a run for it, with Laban's daughters and livestock in tow. There in the desert, where there was no one else for Jacob to bamboozle, the Lord met Jacob. Twice.

The first meeting came in a dream. Jacob dreamed about a grand celestial staircase stretching from heaven to earth. Angels shuttled up and down, and the message couldn't have been clearer. Jacob's emptiness and need would be ferried up, and God's heaped provisions and blessings would be lugged back down.

The second meeting came at dusk by a campfire. The angel of the Lord lunged at him from out of the darkness, and they slugged it out all night. Down in the river, up on the bank. Sand in the eyes, water up the nose. Forehead bruised, ears socked, clumps of hair yanked out. Lips cut and teeth stained red. And finally, a hip de-socketed. Once again, the message couldn't have been plainer. Jacob could no longer grab and run. He would have to lean on Yahweh the way he'd lean on a cane for the rest of his days. Panting, dripping, bleeding, and lame, the swindle was knocked clean out of him, and he got a name change to mark the occasion. From *Jacob to Israel.* From *One Who Takes for Himself* to *Put it on God's Tab.* Or something like that.

The striking thing about the forever and unfailing king identified in Psalm 146 is that he names himself *Jacob's God* (146:5). He calls himself *Jackpot of Swindlers, The One Who Makes Happy Those Who Can't Be Satisfied,* and *The Trust of the Untrusting.*

Living in the ambiguity of Advent, in the waiting, the longing, and the silence, where the shadows and brokenness never seem to let up, and the light barely seems a flicker, it is easy to feel overlooked, left out, forgotten. So, like Jacob, we pass the time with swindles and hustles. But God has not lost track of time nor given up on it. The Gospel story always turns out the same: hustlers who don't trust God try to trick him every chance they get—until their strength runs out. Then they put themselves in God's hands and he cradles them. Or, like Jacob, they fall broken in his arms, and he catches and carries them.

Jesus, our happy trust, will return, and he will bring all he promised. When he does, he may come bounding down Jacob's starlight staircase just for a lark.

Faith and practice: What blessing have you tried to swindle from God? What hustles are you working on now? What would it feel like to lean on grace instead of trying to wring what you want out of Jesus?

Notes

Week 4

GOD BRINGS US THROUGH PROPHECY TO FULFILLMENT THROUGH HIS SON

Isaiah 7:10–16; Psalm 80; Romans 1:1–7; Matthew 1:18–25

DAY 22 – ISAIAH 7:10–16
The Trouble with Signs

When Isaiah was sent to deliver these words to King Ahaz, they were words of salvation—but they were not Christmas words. They were words of hope, but they weren't Joy-to-the-World words. Not yet.

Ahaz had cooked up for himself a particularly sticky political tar pit. The realm-gobbling Assyrians were looking at all the kingdoms in the vicinity and smacking their lips. The northern half of the divided kingdom (Israel) and the nearby kingdom of Aram were trying to press-gang Ahaz's southern half of the divided kingdom (Judah) into a kind of Bible-times NATO to hold the Assyrians off. Ahaz refused the overture, so Israel and Aram sent their best infantry regiments to Jerusalem to force Ahaz's hand.

God sends Isaiah to find Ahaz and deliver good news. "Relax, O King. The plot will fall apart en route. They'll never even make the city limits" (Isaiah 7:4, 7). As icing on the cake, Ahaz is invited to ask for a sign to confirm this word of salvation. Pick a sign, any sign. Ahaz could name his comfort. Ahaz hesitated. Ahaz blushed. "I...I...I couldn't. I wouldn't know what to ask." God bristled at the king's reluctance. It all seems a bit overblown to modern ears. And anyway, isn't there a commandment about not asking for a sign, not putting the Lord to the test? Right, but Ahaz wasn't petitioning; God was offering. Ahaz had already supplied his own sign of salvation, one that didn't require Yahweh's participation at all. Ahaz had just signed a back-room treaty with Assyria, the same superpower that had all the region's monarchs in a cold sweat—and the ink wasn't even dry on the parchment.

Yahweh has the perfect sign to pair with Ahaz's lack of faith. A baby, the birth of a child, but not yet a messiah in a manger. That would be far too great a stretch for a stammering king who couldn't conceive of a sign in real-time. The Messiah would be 700 years down the timeline. For now, a regular, ordinary baby would do. This God loves to use children as signs of his salvation and grace (see Matthew 18). A child is dependent, needy, expectant, and demanding, with outstretched arms and grabbing hands—the very sort of person a God of grace is drawn to! A birth announcement delivered instead of a declaration of war on the eve of catastrophe means that God will be tender toward the vulnerable. We should also point out that this was not a virgin birth. That comes later. The word used here can mean *virgin*, but it can also mean *young woman*. In this case, a young mom will have a baby, but remember, a baby born during an impending invasion means that God is unfolding a gracious future.

It all sounds so ordinary. How will Ahaz know which baby is the sign? The baby will be given a ridiculous name. As a rule, people shouldn't give children biblical or theological names. No way can the kid live up to the namesake. It is bound to end in disappointment. But in this case, it is Yahweh who will live up to the name. Isaiah leaned in and whispered in the king's ear. Ahaz knew how to interpret a name like this, and it was a sermon he wouldn't be able to escape.

But one trouble with signs is that they come in dark seasons. They are meant for perseverance, but we would prefer something else. We would prefer different circumstances. How about just removing all threats of danger and suffering and loss? Wouldn't that be easier? The trouble with signs is that they require faith. What makes every Gospel sign so difficult is also what makes them so beautiful—they keep us reaching, following, and trusting.

God still holds out his salvation to us in signs:

Another birth, this one scandalous and miraculous, in a stable under a phantom star.
A cross filled with a wrongful conviction.
A tomb that lost its grip on its tenant.

A splash of water in the name of Father, Son, and Spirit.
A bite of bread and a swig of wine.
A church left in the world to wear his presence until his return.

They all whisper to us, like Isaiah whispered in the king's ear. God is with us! God adores us! Who can say why, but God adores us!

Our times feel every bit as apocalyptic as Isaiah's. More, even. Nations, kingdoms, and sides still try to hijack God's design while invoking his name. But it never works. God is still unfolding a gracious future to us, and it is whispered in the signs.

Faith and practice: Which of the signs given by Jesus do you take most comfort in? How does it comfort you? Hold on to it. Believe it more than you believe your circumstances and current events.

DAY 23 – ISAIAH 7:10–16
Twice-Named Name

This prophecy was fulfilled twice—once during Isaiah's tenure as prophet to the southern kingdom and once again at the birth of Jesus.

For Isaiah, the prophecy meant that a baby would be born in the south, and for some inexplicable reason, his mother would name him *God with Us*. That birth and that name were a two-sided sign that proclaimed to the people that God was not done with them—no matter how thick their unbelief had grown or how smooth and cunning their disobedience was. A baby meant there was a future, and the name meant there was forgiveness and renewal to go with it.

Seven hundred years later, when Matthew echoes this prophecy in his Gospel, he attaches it to the birth of Jesus (Matthew 1:23). Immanuel, that dirt-smudged little kid running and laughing through the streets of Isaiah's Jerusalem, was a whisper, but Jesus comes like a shout. Here is the fuller fulfillment. This baby isn't just a sign that there will be a future for us; this baby is our future. He will live in our fallenness without falling. He will wear our sentence without a single sin to his own account. He will swim through death from end to end and come wading out of it again. He will erase all holy distance and replace it with holy nearness. It's all written in his name.

That name, worn at two different times, is an unwavering promise. God will not stop until he is with us so that there is no more with-ness left to be had. The nearness to God we so desperately crave, which he craved before us, is expressed and enjoyed exclusively in Jesus. God is with us when we believe Jesus. God is with us when we trust Jesus. God is with us when we rely on Jesus, follow Jesus, and wait for Jesus.

To wear the name Immanuel eternally, Jesus had to return in his second advent. To wear the name to its fullest, he had to return in dawn that

never fades, transforming: exile to homecoming,
hope to presence,
faith to sight,
and perseverance to rejoicing.

The breadth of Scripture can be spoken in a single word: Amen! Baptism is changed to white wedding robes, Eucharist is replaced with a wedding feast, And all our worship grows louder and livelier with the Lamb himself leading the throng.

About that name, Immanuel—there is a third and fuller fulfillment, and it will be soon. Hallelujah!

Faith and practice: Mature Christian living feels like deep contentment and thanksgiving mixed with aching dissatisfaction and longing. In what ways is Jesus with us now? What daily spiritual disciplines help you long for his presence?

DAY 24 – PSALM 80
Grinning Shepherd

When the sheep cry and bleat, the shepherd comes running—staff swinging, club raised, sling whistling overhead. A roused shepherd is bad news for any bear, wolf, lion, or bandit. The charging shepherd is good news for the sheep in distress.

This is a luxuriant Psalm because it revels in the relationship of the shepherd and the sheep. The shepherd saves and keeps, and the sheep cry out, "Give ear! Hear us! Stir up your might! Come quick!" (Psalm 80:1–2). Their cries are like the alarm of a child calling out for a parent. What parent hearing a distress call wouldn't spring into action? Mothers become she-wolves. Fathers turn into berserkers. And the divine shepherd shows up as an avenging God (80:2).

As the Psalmist tells us, the shepherd relishes these saving interventions. He never tires of them; he is a serial savior. So three times, the psalmist cries out, *"Restore"* (80:3, 7, 19). The force of the repetition is undeniable: ee-save, re-save, re-save. And then the psalmist uses the most extravagant word in the psalm: *"again"* (80:14). Do for us what you've done before. Do it another time. And another. God calls this cycle of crying out, intervening, and celebrating by the theological term *worship*.

What's surprising is not the limitless need expressed in the psalm nor the brazenness of asking to be saved repeatedly. It's the divine response: *"Let your face shine, that we may be saved!"* (80:19). Smile upon us, and we will be re-saved.

A shepherd who gives himself to suffer the rejection of the cross and be swallowed by the dense emptiness of the tomb is a shepherd who comes running to save. He scowls at the poachers and rustlers and grins at the flock—even at the strays and the stragglers. Never will his grin shine brighter than when he returns.

Faith and practice: When you cry out to the shepherd, imagine him running out to save, smiling as he does. By the way, this isn't a frivolous or fictional image—it is a biblical self-revelation. Does Jesus's emotional response to our cries change your emotional willingness to send them up?

DAY 25 – ROMANS 1:1–7
Miraculous as Paul

In every town Paul rolled into, new churches seemed to spring up in his footsteps. The great apostle, master church-planter, preaching powerhouse, irresistible revivalist. Paul was the single most successful global evangelist of all time.

Except that's not how Paul tells it. Quoting his own reviews in the local tabloids, Paul says he was known for his *"weighty and strong letters,"* but he wasn't exactly easy on the eyes or ears (2 Corinthians 10:10). And as for his world tours, it's not as if they rolled out the red carpet for him. No, Paul sums up his preaching junket this way: "Five times flogged just shy of death, three times caned, and once stoned. Three times shipwrecked, one of those times a night and day adrift on a chunk of the ship's hull. I've been washed away by rivers, stalked by bandits, and ridden out of town on a rail more times than I can count. I barely sleep, my tongue and lips are dry and cracked, and my stomach always complains about how little it has in it. And I'm always worried about my churches" (2 Corinthians 11:24–27).

As if that weren't enough, Paul says that he was sick for much of his travels (2 Corinthians 12:7), and it was God's idea to give him this affliction so he couldn't be too impressed with himself. We don't know what the diagnosis was exactly, but Paul describes it as a thorn that broke off under the skin and wouldn't give itself to be tweezed out.

Paul didn't even look good on paper. If he wrote up his résumé and sent it off to any church advertising a pastoral vacancy, the whole search committee would laugh themselves red in the face. But thumb through the gold-leaf pages at the back end of any Bible, and you'll glimpse the illogical results of Paul's labor. They were miraculous results: churches at Rome, Colossae, Galatia, Phillipi, and Corinth, to name a few. And more spiritual offspring, through the Gospel, than an Old Testament patriarch—judging by the lists of names that fill the back pages of his letters.

Paul wouldn't bat an eye at the suggestion that the fruit of his ministry was miraculous. He says as much here in the first chapter of Romans: "All of this was promised long ago by the prophets, our being made alive in the Gospel" (1:1-2). "And now he has done it—Jesus has been raised from the dead and declared to be God's Son in power, and he has raised us from the dead with him. He raised me to be an apostle, and he raised you to be saints. But it is God, through Jesus and by the Spirit, who's done the raising" (1:1, 5, 7). That's the thing—we boast in Paul, and we even imagine Paul boasting in himself, but Paul boasts in the Lord. God promised the Gospel. He accomplished it in Jesus, the risen Christ. God gave you the obedience of faith, and me too. God made me an apostle. God made you the church. God made us all servants, says Paul, recipients of grace, love, and peace (1:5, 7).

It is easy for us to doubt that the Gospel will do any good in a world so hostile as ours. Idols and false gods have never been more plentiful. The self-sovereignty of humans exerted in the face of God has never been more defiant and dismissive. Political systems feel beastly and brutal. People seem basely animal in their appetites and prowlings. But Paul never doubted, and his world was every bit as inhospitable. That's what made this apostle—face like a baseball mitt, body broken down like a country road, preaching style that could put the most devout pew sitters to sleep within ten minutes flat—willing to be mistreated in one place, then dust himself off and shamble off to the next. Paul wasn't abused because the Gospel *didn't* work, but because it *did*. He wasn't worked over from town to town because the Gospel lacked power to raise the dead, but because it dripped from heaven with the stuff.

Paul was living proof of the Gospel's power! He wasn't just called to be an apostle, *ex nihilo* (1:1). He had a career, remember? He had status, notoriety, influence, and power. He was an up-and-comer (Acts 8:3). Paul was called *from* something before he was called to something else—from the scourge of the church *to* its greatest apologist and acolyte. So on he slogged to the next place, and the next place, and the next after that—carrying the name that all at once felt heavier than the universe and so light it could lift you right off the ground, burdens and all (1:5). Until one day, Paul walked into Rome and never walked out again. While there, he stepped into a light more phosphorescent and bright than the one that knocked him off his horse on the way to Damascus all those years ago (Acts 9). You get the impression that, if he'd been allowed, Paul would have carried right on until Jesus returned. But now, the God of miracles has called us to carry his name in Paul's place, hasn't he?

Faith and practice: Can you remember the miracle of your faith, belief, conversion, or regeneration? If you have lost touch with your testimony, think back until you get goose flesh and lose your breath for a second at the wonder of God's mercy for you. Visit this memory often.

When you pray for this faith, grace, and conversion for others, do you ask for it as a miracle? Do you confess that it will take a supernatural turning of the heart beyond human effort, endeavor, and willingness? Do you ask that God would be willing to give glory to himself by using someone so ill-fitted as you, just as he did Paul?

DAY 26 – ROMANS 1:1–7
Holy Kiss

This verse reads like a kiss, waking us out of a moment of malaise, soothing us in a season of doubt, or breaking through our perception that God isn't listening anymore—that he has closed and bolted and soundproofed the door on us. We read over these *"grace to you"* verses as if they were just epistolary etiquette. There's not much to them; they just sound good, like something you should say in a churchy letter. But this is the heart of the heavenly Father spilling out through Paul's scribbles. It is us lingering like prodigals at the end of the long driveway, afraid to approach the house for fear of being turned away, when suddenly the door bursts open, and the Father comes barreling out, wrapping us up with laughing tears and kissing the breath out of us. Then, with his face twisted with sobs, beard a wet mess, and eyes running fast like the Jordan River during the spring melt, he pins us to his side with an arm around our shoulder, turning us this way and that, yelling out to the neighbors who are a bit embarrassed at his lack of reserve, "I love no one like I love this one! To its heights and depths, the cosmos cannot measure or contain my love for this one!" The neighbors, red-faced, go back to trimming the hedges, scooping up the morning paper, or watering the flower beds. And the Father? He has more kisses to hand out, and he only stops when he realizes that he has a dinner party to plan.

Grace isn't grace until the best gifts are heaped on the least of the least deserving—with no chance of give-backs. Grace isn't grace unless part of the crowd is scandalized, scornful, and ready to give someone hell to pay for it. But the ones who usually end up paying, sadly, are themselves. Grace, on the other hand, is an unexpected kiss. It's the moment in the wedding ceremony where the officiant asks if anyone has a reason why this knot shouldn't be tied, and a loud rabble files out into the aisle and starts listing all the reasons why. And the groom shrugs and says, "Yeah, but I love her anyway," and he plants on her a kiss fit to be a Hollywood closer. Grace takes things too far. So while a handful of partygoers hurry off with the bride and groom to the reception hall for champagne toasts and the uncorked joy of the dance floor, most of the guests, who can't abide it, stomp off to the parking lot for a committee meeting. Meanwhile, inside the reception hall, another song starts, and the wedding party hoots and cheers. Too far, indeed!

When Paul writes, *"Grace to you and peace from God our Father and the Lord Jesus Christ"* (1:7), he is saying that God is running toward you with open arms. He only has kisses for you. He has hired the hall and the band. He's spread the tables thick, picked up the bar tab, and thinks you'd be a fool not to join him on the dance floor. But he'll mourn your absence if you stay pouting in the parking lot, choking on your merits and entitlements in a self-righteous pity party.

Meanwhile, God's grace is free and plentiful. God draws near to us and reminds us that running low is not the same as running out. He gives us his Spirit and the gifts of fellowship, repentance, forgiveness, charity, and mercy. He gives us our daily bread, sacramental bread, sacramental water, and sacramental word. He listens to our prayers and answers in his perfect sovereignty. He walks beside us along paths of righteousness for his name's sake and fills our hearts with songs. He fills his word with prophecies and promises, the whole lot of them kept. "There's plenty more where that came from! Just wait till we're together!" His parting words may just be enough to cause a few more of us to break off from the parking lot committee and straggle into the dance hall at last.

Faith and practice: Can you believe that everything God gives you, because of Christ Jesus, is a kiss? Try to see it like this—everything he gives you is a kiss, an echo of these words: *"Grace to you and peace."*

DAY 27 – MATTHEW 1:18–25
Betrothed

The scandal was that Mary was found out before she could break the news to Joseph herself (Matthew 1:18). A pregnancy is hard to keep under wraps, and eventually, Mary got bigger around the middle, and the baby was out of the bag, so to speak. But there was a certain beauty to Mary's confounding silence, an admirable faith in her refusal to try to explain. There was no Marian damage control, no trying to get ahead of the thing, no trying to soften the blow. Her sheer trust is remarkable. This is God's doing, so let him explain it himself.

And explain it Joseph did—but not before allowing himself to sink into considerable distress. Joseph knew how these things worked, and he knew that Mary's growing waistline had not been his work. Her story was inventive; he had to give her that—but it was hardly plausible. Certainly not something he could tell the guys in town. They'd laugh him clear out of Nazareth. Joseph felt sick to his stomach, felt his chest tightening, and had trouble catching his breath. He couldn't eat. He couldn't sleep. His head throbbed and spun with scenarios. How? Who? Why?

His co-workers were starting to worry about him. He'd hung a lintel crooked and smashed his thumb with a hammer, and he often stood in the middle of the job site adrift in some private trouble. At lunch, he'd sit by himself under an olive tree, not even bothering to unroll it and have a look. His puffy eyes sagged heavier than his bag of tools. Eventually, the head of the carpenters' union suggested he take some time off. Get sorted. His job would be waiting for him when he got back.

Later, Joseph knew what he had to do. It was honorable and decent, and no one would blame him. And it was right by Mary. Whatever she'd done, he did love her. This felt loving in its own way—it would spare her having to pin a red A to her dress. It would preserve some dignity for her and allow her to build a life for herself and the baby. And maybe, if he spotted her pushing a stroller through the village from time to time, he would squeeze out a small smile, knowing she was well, knowing what he'd done for her. Divorce. He'd call his lawyer tomorrow. See to it quietly. That night, Joseph slept for the first time in weeks, like a man for whom all was right in the world. Only it wasn't.

What did Joseph dream that night? It's hard to explain. He dreamed that the angel of the Lord said to him, "New plan, which is actually the same old plan," and he explained that Joseph wouldn't be putting Mary away after all. He would go through with the marriage as arranged, and he'd have to get a nursery ready. Mary was telling the truth. The baby that grew inside her was from the Holy Spirit. Oh, and one more thing. The child was not to be named Joseph. He was to be named after his father, "So call him *One Who Saves*," the angel directed. Then the angel left, Joseph woke up, or both (Matthew 1:20–23).

In this strange, lovely little story, the Gospel couldn't be more straightforward. God does not put us away, quietly or otherwise. We are betrothed. We are reserved to belong to him. We are also adulterers. We take up with every rival suitor that comes along—roving eyes, roving hearts, roving faith, roving trust. And yet, God does not divorce us. He does not turn away. He does the opposite. He weds us. It's in his name, after all, One Who Saves. We are married to one we don't deserve, but one who refuses to abandon us, and all our shame melts away. So does any sense that we don't belong to him. No room to bring shame or unbelief into the marriage! In our long betrothal and our long wait for the Groom to arrive, we have this story as an assurance. He refuses to put us away and insists on drawing us close. If we lose sight of it as we wait (and we are bound to lose sight of it), his refusal to leave us is in his name (1:21, 23). *He is near.* He must be.

The following morning, Joseph got up, drank a cup of coffee, brushed his teeth, combed his hair, and oiled his beard. He put on his best tunic, walked to the corner, bought a small bouquet of flowers, and rang Mary's doorbell. When she opened the door, she saw the Gospel standing on the stoop.

Faith and practice: What kinds of circumstances do you encounter in life that trick you into thinking, "Well, maybe he isn't coming back?" What could you use from Matthew 1:18–25 to argue those doubts into silence?

DAY 28 - MATTHEW 1:18-25
Three Things

By the time Joseph had shaken himself awake from his bleary dream, he knew three things for sure.

1. He was not to divorce Mary.
2. Mary's child had been conceived by the Holy Spirit.
3. The child's name was to be Jesus, *One Who Saves*.

Everything else was a holy mystery. Each year, when we unbox our crèches for another holiday, there isn't much mystery left. Because we live on the far side of the story, we see the entire Gospel drama in the little figures, even though they are frozen at the start. We delight in the beginning because we already know the end. But Joseph didn't have that luxury. There was so much Joseph couldn't see. So much Joseph couldn't know. Imagine the questions.

"Why Mary? Why me? How has this come to us? How will we raise a God-child? What if we fail? How will we train and prepare him?" There must have been dozens more. "His name is to be *One Who Saves*? We are to call him *Long-Awaited Savior*? How will that go over? What will people say? Family? Neighbors? The rabbi? The Romans? How will he be received?" Joseph could easily have fallen into Abraham's mistake here—no sooner had God made his promise to Abraham that Abraham busied himself trying to bring about God's promise on his own.

But Joseph knew three things. They were a beacon to follow, the light in the dark. Joseph believed the word of the Lord just as Mary had months before. It is pointed out in the passage with a glorious understatement: *"When Joseph woke from sleep, he did as the angel of the Lord commanded him"* (1:24). The way to not be lost in the anxious unknown of mystery is to follow what we know—what is spoken, written, and passed down from the Lord.

Think of the questions that judge, mock, and harass us today. They plague us in our exile and almost drag us away from watching and waiting for Christ's return. How much longer? Why hasn't he come yet? What stands in the way? Is he truly coming, or have we been swindled? Hustled? Had?

Maybe our questioning and doubt are a different variety. Maybe we don't doubt that he is coming back, but we want some assurances about this meantime we are marooned in. We want some insider information about what we can expect for the remainder of our wait. What's ahead? What's coming? How bad will it get? How hard? Will it hurt? Will our faith and confession hold up or crumble? Will we thrive or languish? We can't know any of this—no matter how much we pace and wring our hands. We can be swept away by circumstances and intimidated by our ignorance, or we can walk in the Gospel. We've been given a beacon to follow, just like Joseph:

1. Jesus will not divorce us and has not put us away.
2. Sustaining faith has been conceived in us by the Holy Spirit.
3. Jesus will live up to his name and return again soon!

What stands between us and our wedding day, the day of redemption and eternal joy, is hidden behind a dark curtain we cannot peer behind.

But we know three things.

Faith and practice: What do you think you need to make the waiting in exile more tolerable? Less distressing and anxious? More assured? Can you let go of those things, and cling to these three? Use these three things to fight the terror of the darkness with the confidence of faith.

Notes

www.ingramcontent.com/pod-product-compliance
Lightning Source LLC
Chambersburg PA
CBHW041131110526
44592CB00020B/2762